SEVEN ANIMALS
WAG THEIR TALES

Retold by Howard I. Bogot and Mary K. Bogot
Illustrated by Fred Marvin

PITSPOPANY

NEW YORK ◆ JERUSALEM

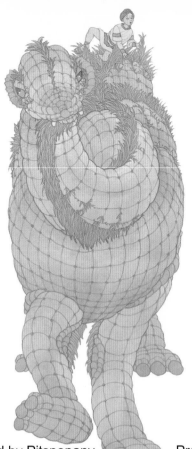

Published by Pitspopany Press
Text Copyright © 2000 by Howard I. Bogot and Mary K. Bogot
Illustrations Copyright © 2000 by Fred Marvin

Design: Tiffen Studios (T.C. Peterseil)

PITSPOPANY PRESS books may be purchased for educational or
special sales by contacting:

  Marketing Director, Pitspopany Press
  40 East 78th Street, Suite 16D
  New York, New York 10021
  Tel: 1-800-232-2931
  Fax: (212) 472-6253
  E-mail: pop@netvision.net.il
  Web: www.pitspopany.com

ISBN: 1-930143-00-1 Cloth
ISBN: 1-930143-01-X Paper

Printed in Hong Kong

CONTENTS

THEME	STORY	

THEME	STORY	
TEAMWORK	The Wiggle That Could Slice Stone	6
COOPERATION	Giant Og And The Ant Cave	12
ACCEPTING DIFFERENCES	Duncan The Talking Donkey	18
DUTY	Saved By The King Of Beasts	24
HELPFULNESS	The Hoopoe Bird Helps Sly Fox	30
COURAGE	Barkus The Sheepdog Learns A Lesson	36
MAKING CHOICES	Meepul - Yupul Pull The Ark	42

ALSO AVAILABLE IN THIS SERIES:

Seven Animal Stories For Children
Seven Delightful Stories For Every Day

Ages 3-6

The Wiggle That Could Slice Stone

Working together is a great way to get things done

Mother," the baby Shamir worms asked, "Why does everyone call you a hero?"

"Well, little ones," their mother answered, "it all started when King Solomon wanted to build the most beautiful Temple that had ever been built."

King Solomon selected huge pieces of magnificent Jerusalem stone that would be cut into blocks, polished and fitted together.

The royal stonecutters hammered on the stones trying to cut them to just the right size. All day long, from sunrise until sunset, you could hear their tools making loud noises: *Boom!*

Slam!

Clack!

Ping!

Thud!

By the time they arrived home, they hardly had enough strength to eat their dinner. All they wanted to do was sleep.

This went on day after day after day and the tired stonecutters began to grumble.

"I don't know how much longer I can swing my hammer."

"These stones are too hard and thick."

"When will we have time for our families?"

Hearing them grumble, I turned to your aunts, uncles and cousins and said, "These folks are trying to do what is almost impossible for them, but simple for us. We were created with bodies that can work magic when we're placed on a stone."

Two of your cousins stretched a vine in a straight line across one of the biggest stones. Then I wiggled back and forth along that line. It was great fun.

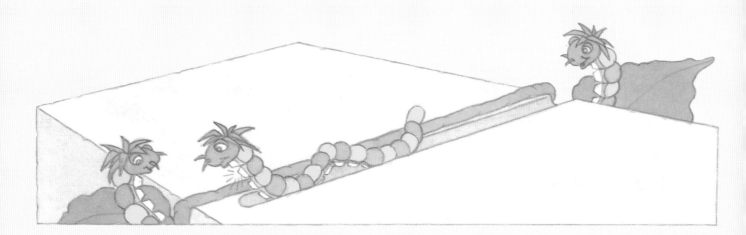

One of the workmen saw what I was doing and brushed his hand over the stone to chase me away. But as soon as he touched the stone, it split apart into two perfect halves.

"Wow! Look what these worms can do," the stonecutters exclaimed when they saw how quickly we split the stone. "It's magic."

Soon we were working together, we Shamirs cutting the stones and the stonecutters using their special talents to chisel and fit the stones together.

The stonecutters were not so tired any more. They even had time for their families.

The stonecutters took good care of us. They found tasty leaves for us to eat and built soft nests for us to rest in during the day. The king was amazed at the progress the stonecutters were making. He rewarded them with higher wages and family vacations.

But even with our help, it took the stonecutters many years to build the Temple just the way King Solomon wanted.

When the Temple was completed, King Solomon led a large parade through the streets and invited the stonecutters and their families to be his special guests.

And the stonecutters invited us to be *their* special guests. On a large stone, high enough for us to watch the festivities, they threw us the best *Wiggly Party* your relatives and I have ever attended.

Then they shouted,

"Shamirs, you will always be our heroes!"

THINKING THOUGHTS

* How did the stonecutters and the Shamirs help each other?
* In what games or sports do you need teamwork in order to succeed?
* How does your family work together like a team?

Giant Og And The Ant Cave

Sometimes God uses the littlest creatures to make the greatest miracles

I was just about to carry a heavy bread crumb home for dinner, when I heard a very loud voice coming from the Israelite campsite.

"Moses, we must run away!" shouted one of the Israelites. "We're in great danger! The giant, Og, is coming to do battle with us. He's just one day's walk away. The earth is already shaking beneath our feet."

A crowd gathered and everyone began talking at once.

"The giant, Og, is twenty-four miles tall," said one person.

"Twenty-four miles? That's higher than Mount Sinai," said another.

"We will be like ants to him. He will crush us!" said yet a third.

12

Moses didn't want the people to run away. So, while he was thinking of what to do, Moses started singing,

"Who's afraid of the big, mean Og?
Who's afraid of Og?
God said, 'Don't be afraid of the big mean Og,'
So, I'm not afraid of Og!"

Soon, everyone joined in. They were singing, but they were still scared.

As I listened to the singing, I heard the sound of Og's footsteps growing louder and louder. The ground shook so strongly that I was almost knocked off my feet. It was then I called a meeting of all the ants in the kingdom.

"We must find a way to save the Israelites before Og and his army get here," I explained. "Og will not only crush the Israelites, he will crush us too."

One of the ants heard that Og's feet were so big and heavy that he needed to rest very often.

"He always rests on the top of a hill," she said.

"Call all the ants together from all the nearby lands," I ordered. "We may be tiny creatures, but working together, we can make a difference."

Soon, I was surrounded by an army of ants. As Moses and the Israelites slept, or tried to sleep, we set about building a giant anthill. We only had a few hours to do it in, but we were certain that if we worked together all night long, we could do it.

By morning, the anthill was complete. Then we carefully removed the dirt from inside the ant hill, so that the anthill was hollow. We had built an *ant cave.*

"Og is coming!" someone in the Israelite camp shouted. Everyone began to run away. We hid inside an old tree stump. When the giant, Og, reached the camp of the Israelites, he bellowed, "I'm exhausted. Before I stomp on these little people, I must find a place to rest."

Og sat down on our tall ant cave.

BOOOOOOOOM!

The ant cave caved in. Down fell Og, deeper and deeper into the ant cave. He tried to get up, but thousands of us quickly threw sand on him. Every time he tried to rise, he would slip on the loose sand.

I crawled up onto Moses' hand and reported, "Og cannot get out of the hole. The dirt and sand are too loose. Lead your people to safety."

Gently, Moses put me back on the ground.

But, before he led the Israelites to safety, he said to them:

"Remember that sometimes the smallest of God's creatures can bring about the greatest of miracles."

THINKING THOUGHTS

* Besides singing, what do you think Moses did while waiting for Og to attack?
* How do you think the ants were able to create such a big hole so quickly?
* What can you do when you work with other people, that you can't do by yourself?

Duncan The Talking Donkey

Being different doesn't mean you can't be friends

When Balaam and I were very young, we used to romp together in the fields. We were two good friends who enjoyed each other's company.

But all the camels and horses made fun of me.

"Balaam's not an animal like you are," they would say. "He's a stranger to our way of life. You shouldn't be playing with him."

I knew that Balaam and I were very different. He was a stranger to my donkey life and I was a stranger to his human life, but we didn't care.

As Balaam got older, Balaam's family and friends began to notice that he had magical powers. Some people believed that God spoke to him, but other people thought he was just strange.

I never questioned Balaam's behavior, except once when the Israelites set up a large, tent camp near King Balak's neighborhood.

King Balak told Balaam, "I want you to place a curse on the Israelites and chase them out of our neighborhood. They're not like us. They're strangers. They make us feel uncomfortable."

Balaam agreed with King Balak and soon I was trotting off with Balaam on my back heading to the place where the Israelites were camped. But, when we got close, an angel of God stepped in front of me. I understood why he was there and I wouldn't go any further. But Balaam didn't see the angel at all.

"At this rate, Duncan," Balaam complained impatiently, kicking me on my sides, "I could walk faster."

"So, why don't you?" I replied.

"Duncan, it's a miracle! You can talk! Why haven't you ever spoken before?"

19

"Balaam," I replied, "since we were children I've been very proud to be your friend. But, today, you could make the biggest mistake of your life. So, I just had to speak out."

"But the Israelites are strangers," Balaam shouted, "I must chase them away." Then he gave me a WHAACK with his stick and commanded, "Now let's get moving."

For the first time I was angry at Balaam and with a loud hee-haw I kicked up my legs and bounced him onto the ground.

"Balaam," I said, "when we started spending time together, the other animals said you were a stranger to our way of life, but we played together and became friends. And when you grew up, some people thought you were strange and stayed away from you. Well, the Israelites may be strangers to King Balak, but we're all strangers to someone."

"Duncan, who do you think you are?" Balaam angrily answered. "I'm an important person and I can make my own decisions. I know what God wants. Now take me to the hilltop overlooking the Israelite's camp."

This time I knew I better do what I was told.

Balaam and I climbed to the top of the hill and looked down at the Israelites. He looked out over the desert where the Israelites were camped. Suddenly, a strange glow spread over his face.

Balaam spread his hands wide and said, "How wonderful are your tents, Children of Jacob; how wonderful are your homes, Children of Israel."

I know I heard what Balaam said. I was there. I just wonder: What changed his mind?

THINKING THOUGHTS

* What do you think changed Balaam's mind about the Israelites?
* What did Duncan mean when he said "we're all strangers to someone"?
* When a new child comes to class, how do you make him or her feel like a friend?

Saved By The King Of Beasts

Everyone should take their job in life seriously

I love being called King of the Beasts. Of course, it's not *all* fun. I have many responsibilities too. The animals expect me to chase the hyenas, because they're always laughing and being a nuisance. The deer, gazelles, water buffalo and sheep all want me to give up my meat diet and eat more vegetables. I'm sure you can guess why.

And, my wife, Mrs. Roarsom, wants me to help her take care of our lion cubs and insists that I keep my mane combed.

But, being called King of the Beasts has its rewards too. As a matter of fact, it once helped me save King David, when he was a shepherd boy.

Young David never lost a sheep. He knew how to chase away hyenas and wolves, and even me, the King of the Beasts.

One day, David decided to climb up what appeared to be a steep hill. He wanted to sit right on the very top so that he could watch his flock of sheep while he relaxed and ate his lunch.

As he got to the top of the hill, the ground beneath his feet started to shake. Too late, David realized that the hill he had climbed was not a hill at all. It was the back of a great beast called the *Re'em*. The Re'em had been asleep and now it began to move about. It stood up and stretched.

The Re'em was VERY, VERY tall. David held on to the hairs on the back of the Re'em as tightly as he could.

"How am I going to get back down to my flock?" David thought to himself.

The Re'em started to take a walk. Soon, David would be miles away from his flock.

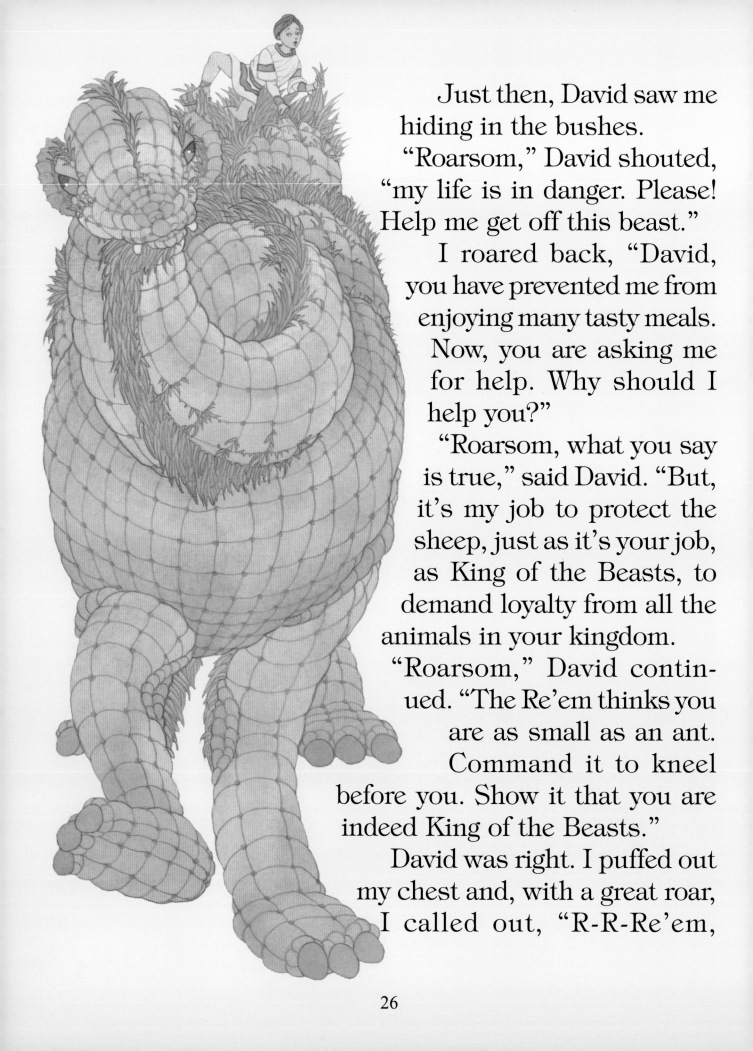

Just then, David saw me hiding in the bushes.

"Roarsom," David shouted, "my life is in danger. Please! Help me get off this beast."

I roared back, "David, you have prevented me from enjoying many tasty meals. Now, you are asking me for help. Why should I help you?"

"Roarsom, what you say is true," said David. "But, it's my job to protect the sheep, just as it's your job, as King of the Beasts, to demand loyalty from all the animals in your kingdom.

"Roarsom," David continued. "The Re'em thinks you are as small as an ant. Command it to kneel before you. Show it that you are indeed King of the Beasts."

David was right. I puffed out my chest and, with a great roar, I called out, "R-R-Re'em,

26

kneel down before me. I am your King. I am R-R-Roarsom, King of the Beasts."

The Re'em looked down. Slowly, it bowed low, so low that David was able to slide safely to the ground.

"Roarsom," David shouted as he ran towards his flock, "you are indeed King of the Beasts. If ever I am king, I will give you your own land where no one will be permitted to chase you. This I promise."

And sure enough, when David became king he gave me my own land. And since then, no one has ever chased me, not even my friend, King David.

THINKING THOUGHTS

* **What were the jobs of David and Roarsom?**
* **Why didn't Roarsom want David to do his job?**
* **Why do you think the giant Re'em bowed to the King of the Beasts?**
* **What jobs do you have during the day?**

The Hoopoe Bird Helps Sly Fox

*Sometimes you should do the right thing,
even if you don't want to*

When I was a very young birdie, Grandpa Hoopoe told me that Hoopoes can see water deep down in the ground as easily as a person can see through glass. Grandpa said that we Hoopoes even helped many of the ancient Israelites find water when they were walking in the hot, dusty, desert sun.

One day, when I was all grown up, I was sitting in a tree with my Hoopoe family when, all of a sudden, everyone started flapping their wings and shrieking, "Hoop! Hoop! Hoop!" I looked around and saw Sly, the fox, coming toward us.

Sly and the members of his family have been chasing the members of my family for as long as I can remember. But, this time, things were very different. This time Sly didn't chase me. Instead, he looked up at me and spoke with tears in his eyes.

30

"Hoopoe, I need your help. It's very hot and dry where we live. Our spring has dried up and our newborn baby foxes are so thirsty that they may die. I've heard that Hoopoes can find water. Could you fly over and find some water for us? Please!"

Help Sly? My common sense told me that Sly was an enemy and it was not in his nature to ever become my friend. Should I help him?

I quickly flew over to the tree house of Knowit, the wise owl, and woke him up from his daytime sleep. "What's all the commotion?" he hooted, still half asleep. "I've been up all night. Can't an old owl get some rest?"

"I'm sorry, Knowit, but I need your advice." Then I told him my problem.

"Hoopoe, I think that the learned teachers of the Israelites wrote an answer to your question in one of their wonderful books.

If your enemy arrives at your home, hungry and thirsty, give him food and drink."

Knowit scratched his head with his wing, thinking for a moment before he spoke, "I suggest that you act with goodness and show kindness, but protect yourself at the same time."

"Thank you, Knowit, now I know what to do."

As I settled into my nest, I chirped to Sly, "Okay, I'll help you."

I flew high above Sly as he raced back to his family. Then I flew round and round. Sure enough, beneath a big bush not far from his cave, I saw a stream of water.

"I really can find water, I really can! Grandpa Hoopoe was right." I shouted down to Sly, "Ask your neighbors to dig deep beneath that big bush. You'll find plenty of water there."

Sly, and the Fox family, four raccoons and two brown bears dug and dug and dug. Dirt and stones were flying everywhere. Then, just before sunset, a fountain

of fresh water rushed up from the ground. Water spilled over in every direction for the baby foxes and all the thirsty animals.

Flying home, I wondered if Sly would ever be my friend, but I felt good that I had helped him. After all, what can be more important than saving the lives of God's creatures?

THINKING THOUGHTS

* How did Knowit the owl help Hoopoe save the fox family?
* Why did Hoopoe feel good even though Sly would probably never be his friend?
* When have you helped someone who you knew wasn't your friend?

Barkus The Sheepdog Learns A Lesson

When there's no one to help, then it's up to you to do your best

Before my master, Moses, led the Israelites from slavery to freedom, he was just a simple shepherd and I was his sheepdog.

Moses named me Barkus because, when I was a puppy, I would run after the lambs, barking. The lambs would romp in every direction, bleating, "Bah! Bah! Bah!" It was a great game.

But the shepherds did not think it was a game. Each time they were sure that my barking was a signal that the lambs were being attacked by some hungry animal and they would come running to save their flocks. When they discovered that I was causing all the noise, they scolded me, but I didn't stop barking.

I barked at the lambs. I barked at the mice. I barked at the cats and even at the butterflies. After many false alarms, the shepherds stopped running to the rescue. Instead, they complained about me to Moses.

Moses scolded me, but he was always kind and forgiving. He would pet me and say, "Barkus, protecting the lives of the lambs is a very important job because they can't care for themselves. They depend on you to keep them safe. You must learn not to chase them with your barking."

One day, as I was trotting through the meadows, I heard a loud, "Grrrrr!" Then a louder, "Grrrrr" and "Bah! Bah! Bah!" A hungry wolf was running towards the little, young lambs. The wolf's mouth was open and I could see his teeth. I was scared, but the lambs were even more frightened.

All the sheep were bleating for help and I started howling and barking as loud as I could....WOOF! WOOF! AWOO! AWOO! WOOF! But the shepherds didn't come. "Oh, NO!" I thought, "The shepherds think I'm chasing the lambs or barking at a butterfly."

"It's no use," I barked to the lambs. "Let's run away," and I started running as fast as I could. Suddenly, I skidded to a stop. "Wait, Barkus," I said to myself. "Caring for the lambs is your responsibility." I turned around and raced back to the flock as fast as I could. Moses was running toward the flock, too. He had a big stick in his hand.

"Shoo! Shoo!" Moses shouted, waving the stick at the wolf.

"Woof! Woof! Woof!" I barked in my loudest voice. We were working

38

together like a real team. It didn't take long before the wolf put its tail between its legs and ran away.

I was dusty, thirsty and more tired than I had ever been.

"Barkus," Moses said, patting me on the head, "saving the lambs took a lot of courage. Today you made me very proud of you."

Moses and I led the lambs to safety and then Moses took me home, bathed me and gave me some fresh, cool water from the well to drink. I felt exhausted on the outside, but *inside*, I felt very good. I felt like barking for joy!

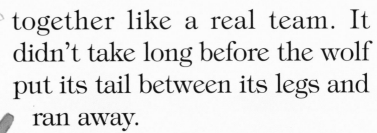

THINKING THOUGHTS

* Why do you think Barkus turned back to protect the flock of sheep?
* Why did Barkus feel like "barking for joy"?
* When did you help someone all by yourself?

Meepul - Yupul
Pull The Ark

Making the right choice is not always easy

Meepul and Yupul were resting in the tall cool grass watching the new young calves with their mothers on the far hillside. Once, they were young, strong cows. But now, Meepul and her sister, Yupul, were quite old, but they were still loved by the Israelites.

"Yupul, tell me again why we're grazing in a field in the land of the Israelites? Don't we belong to the Philistines?"

"Meepul, how many times must I tell you about the Ark and the big battle between the Israelites and the Philistines?" Yupul replied.

"Remind me just one more time, Yupul, please. One more time and I promise to not forget."

"Very well, one last time."

42

Many years ago, the Philistines waged a fierce battle against the Israelites. The Philistines wanted more land and with their mighty army they were certain that they would win.

The Israelites were having a hard time. The enemy was advancing and no help seemed to be in sight. "We must bring the Holy Ark that holds the tablets of the Ten Commandments into our camp," said the leaders of the Israelites. "Only the Ark can give our people the courage and the confidence they need to beat the Philistines."

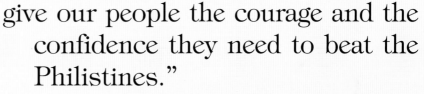

As soon as the Ark arrived, the Israelite soldiers began to cheer and tears of joy streamed down their cheeks.

Now it was the Philistines' turn to worry. "We must get that Ark away from the Israel-ites," they agreed. So, in a sudden surprise attack, the Philistines stole the Ark.

The Philistines ran with the Ark back to their camp and placed it next to the giant statue of their hero god, Dagon. But, in the morning, they found Dagon had fallen over and its head was lying in front of the Ark.

The Philistines realized that terrible things would happen if they didn't give the Ark back to the Israelites. "We must return the Ark to the Israelites before we're destroyed," they declared.

The Philistines quickly put the Ark on a large cart. "We will select our two best cows, Meepul and Yupul, to pull the cart and we will put many gifts in the Ark."

Meepul and Yupul did not want to leave their calves and their cow friends. But the young calves said to their mothers: "We know you love us and we know it will be hard to leave us, but we're

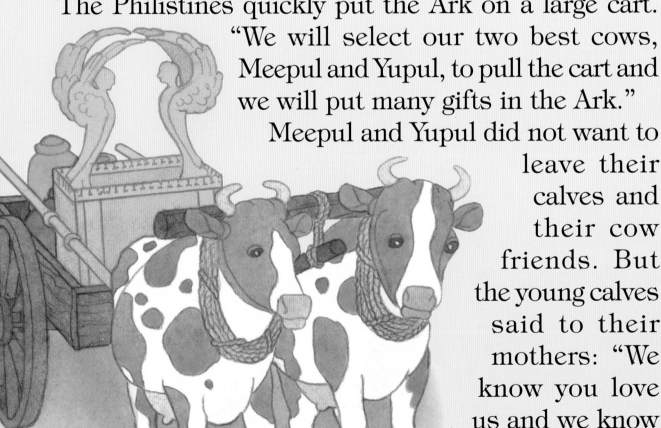

growing up and we'll be fine. You have a chance for a new and important life. Return the Ark to the Israelites. That's where it belongs."

"Those two cows were you and me," Yupul said to her sister.

"When we arrived here in Bayt Shemesh with the Ark, the Israelites cheered and danced. Celebrations were held for days.

"From that day on, the Israelites have looked after us and given us these beautiful hills to graze on."

THINKING THOUGHTS

* **What choices did the Israelites and the Philistines make in this story?**
* **What do you think makes the Ark so important?**
* **Why do you think Meepul and Yupul made their difficult choice?**

SEVEN ANIMAL STORIES FOR CHILDREN

Stories By Theme:
Respect   Modesty
Gratitude   Honesty
Attitude   Friendship
Responsibility

SEVEN DELIGHTFUL STORIES FOR EVERY DAY

Stories By Theme:
Modesty   Patience
Respect   Hospitality
Kindness   Responsibility
Attitude